THIS BOOK
belongs to

.... name

nutri·edu·kids
WWW.NUTRIEDUKIDS.COM

Copyright 2022 Nutri Edu Kids Ltd.
ISBN 9798360006862
www.nutriedukids.com

FOR CAREGIVERS

Welcome to "All About Vitamins"!

LEARN TOGETHER

Dive into the world of vitamins! Read and discuss their benefits, explore foods rich in the vitamin you're learning about.
Let this activity book ignite meaningful conversations about the significance of nutrition.

COOK TOGETHER

Studies have shown that kids who are frequently involved in the cooking process feel more in control and become more adventurous eaters! Let's create lasting memories and develop a love for diverse foods by cooking as a team!

BE CREATIVE TOGETHER

Unleash your culinary imagination with custom recipes from this activity book. Cook as a team, select your favorite ingredients, and craft your unique recipes!

OUR MISSION

Our mission is to provide valuable resources for parents and kids, inspiring and facilitating conversations about nutrition. Together, let's sow the seeds of a healthier and happier future!

 IF YOU WANT TO MAKE LEARNING EVEN MORE ENGAGING, CHECK OUT OUR **FREE VIDEO COURSE FOR KIDS:** "ALL ABOUT VITAMINS" ON OUR YOUTUBE CHANNEL: Go to https://www.youtube.com/@nutriedukids/playlists

Watch as the information from the book comes to life in our videos, helping kids remember important facts with fun visuals.

COLOR YOUR

FAVORITE

FOODS!

color me!

peanut butter

4

DID YOU KNOW THAT EVERY FOOD HAS ITS UNIQUE HEALTH BENEFITS? LET'S EXPLORE THE COLORFUL WORLD OF VITAMINS!

YOU PROBABLY ALREADY KNOW THAT EATING *healthy* IS IMPORTANT, RIGHT?

BUT DO YOU KNOW WHAT "HEALTHY" REALLY MEANS? *Let's find out!*

Well, it means eating foods that are good for your body!

Foods contain nutrients

that our body needs every day. Just like how a car needs fuel to work, your body needs these special nutrients from foods every day to be its best! So, let's explore what these nutrients are and where we can find them!

6

Vitamins

ARE A TYPE OF THESE NUTRIENTS THAT CAN BE FOUND
IN THE FOODS YOU EAT. WE NEED TO

get vitamins from food every day

BECAUSE OUR BODY CAN NOT PRODUCE THEM

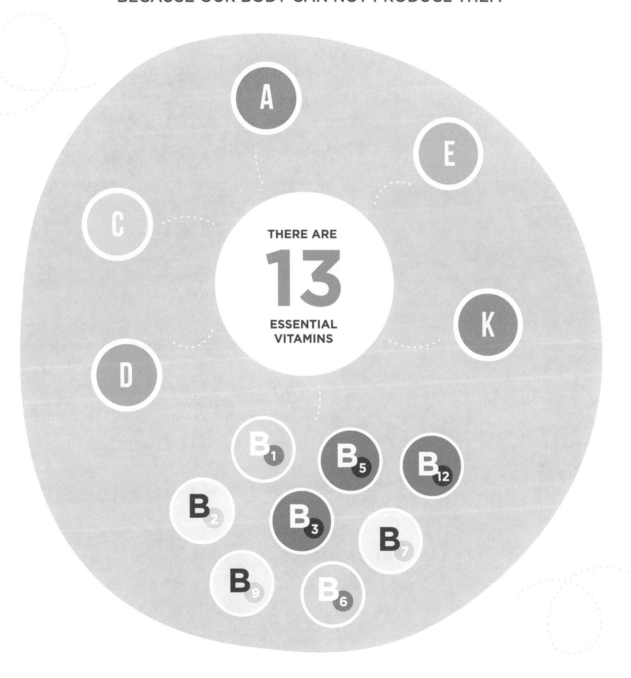

There are 13 essential vitamins:

A, C, D, E, K, AND THE EIGHT B VITAMINS.

THERE ARE TWO DIFFERENT TYPES OF VITAMINS: FAT-SOLUBLE
AND WATER-SOLUBLE. THIS DIFFERENCE DECIDES HOW THE
BODY STORES AND TRANSPORTS VITAMINS.

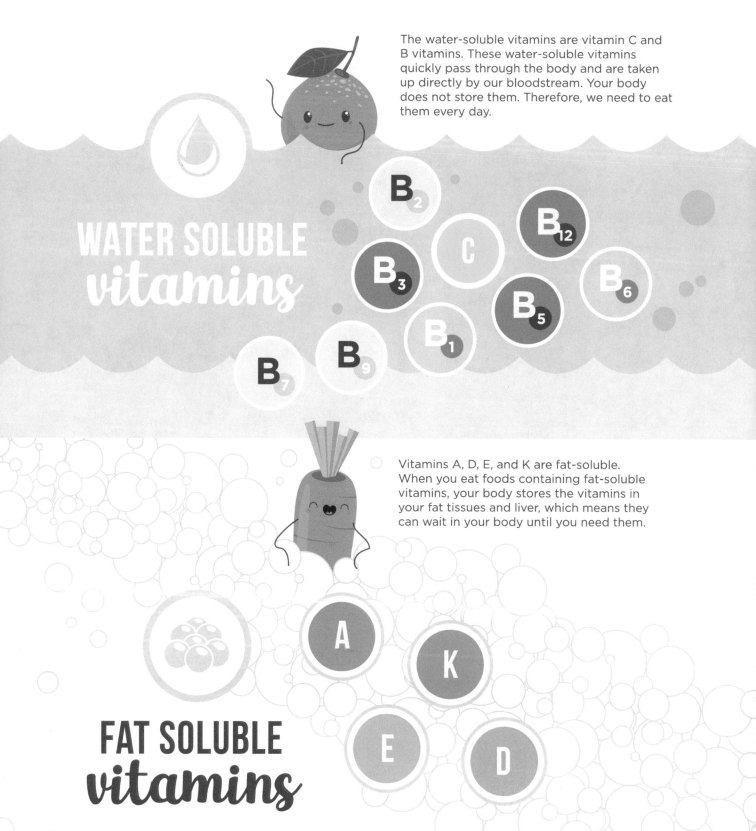

The water-soluble vitamins are vitamin C and
B vitamins. These water-soluble vitamins
quickly pass through the body and are taken
up directly by our bloodstream. Your body
does not store them. Therefore, we need to eat
them every day.

WATER SOLUBLE
vitamins

B₂ B₁₂ C B₃ B₆ B₅ B₁ B₇ B₉

Vitamins A, D, E, and K are fat-soluble.
When you eat foods containing fat-soluble
vitamins, your body stores the vitamins in
your fat tissues and liver, which means they
can wait in your body until you need them.

A K E D

FAT SOLUBLE
vitamins

DO YOU KNOW WHAT
the health benefits
OF EACH VITAMIN ARE?

EACH VITAMIN HAS ITS OWN
special superpower
TO HELP YOUR BODY BE STRONG AND HEALTHY:

Vitamin A helps your **vision**.

Vitamins A, C and E give you a **strong immune system**. Your immune system is like a shield that protects you from getting ill and also helps you recover from diseases.

Vitamin K improves your **healing after injury**.

B vitamins help you to be **more energetic, active and strong**.

Vitamin D helps to maintain **healthy bones**.

LET'S LEARN MORE
about vitamins!
WE'LL FIND OUT HOW THEY CAN HELP YOU AND
discover the foods
WHERE YOU CAN FIND THEM!

Plant Powered
VITAMIN A
NUTRITION EDUCATION FOR KIDS

FUN EXERCISES | ALL ABOUT VITAMIN A | SUNSHINE SMOOTHIE RECIPE

The Health Benefits of
VITAMIN A

DID YOU KNOW?

The most important benefit of Vitamin A: it improves night vision, protects eyes from disease, and keeps them healthy

GOOD

VISION

HEALTHY
SKIN AND HAIR

STRONG
IMMUNE SYSTEM

STRONG
BONES AND TEETH

FOODS THAT CONTAIN
VITAMIN A

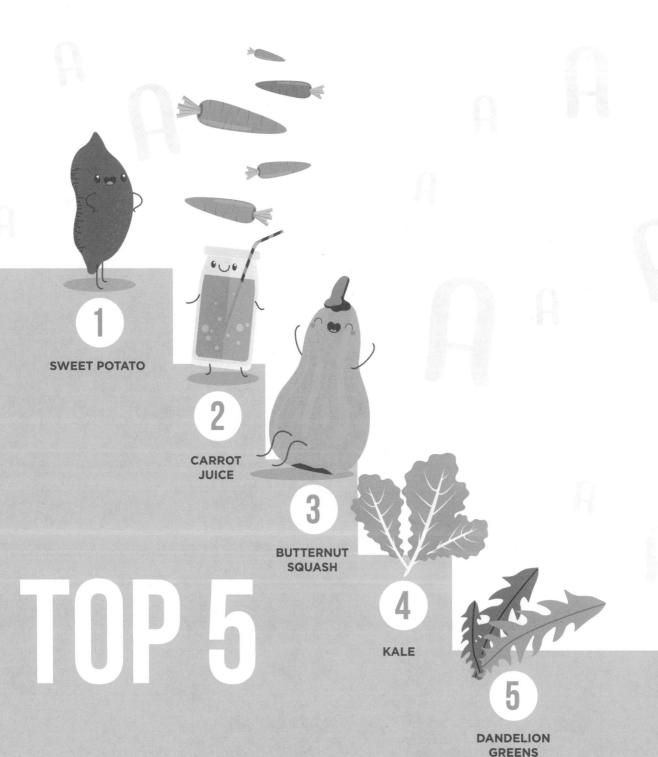

1 SWEET POTATO

2 CARROT JUICE

3 BUTTERNUT SQUASH

4 KALE

5 DANDELION GREENS

TOP 5

COLOR
VITAMIN A FOODS!

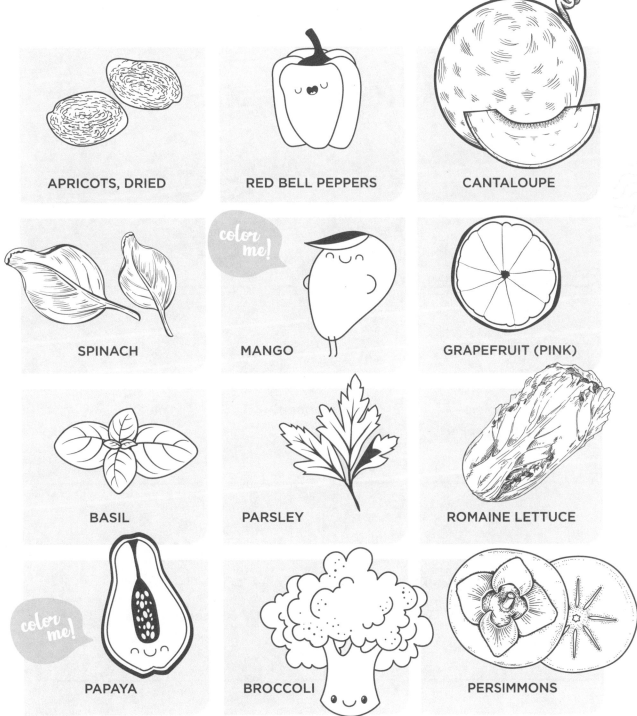

APRICOTS, DRIED

RED BELL PEPPERS

CANTALOUPE

SPINACH

color me! MANGO

GRAPEFRUIT (PINK)

BASIL

PARSLEY

ROMAINE LETTUCE

color me! PAPAYA

BROCCOLI

PERSIMMONS

How much
IN ONE DAY?

You get your vitamin A necessary for the day if you eat one of these:

Choose one:

   +

**1/4 cup
dried apricots**
          **1/2 cup diced 
cantaloupe**

or

   +   + 

**1 medium
red bell pepper**
    **1 cup chopped 
spinach**
    **1 medium
mango**

or

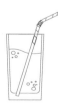   **1/2 cup
carrot juice**

or

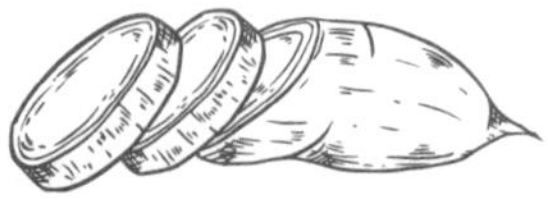

**1/2 cup cooked, mashed
sweet potato**

Create your own Vitamin A smoothie by choosing one ingredient of each color! Pick all your chosen ingredients and combine them on the recipe card (next page)!

CUSTOMIZE YOUR OWN VITAMIN A
SUNSHINE SMOOTHIE!

choose one
PICK YOUR LIQUID*:

1 CUP APPLE JUICE

1 CUP ORANGE JUICE

1 CUP PEACH JUICE

choose one
PICK YOUR VITAMIN A:

1/2 CUP PAPAYA

1/2 CUP CANTALOUPE

1/2 CUP CHOPPED CARROT

choose one
PICK YOUR BASE*:

1/2 CUP FROZEN BANANA

1/2 CUP FROZEN MANGO

1/2 CUP FROZEN PINEAPPLE

choose one
SPICE IT UP:

1 TABLESPOON LEMON JUICE

1 TABLESPOON LIME JUICE

optional:
BOOST YOUR SMOOTHIE WITH HEALTHY FATS:

chia

1 TEASPOON OF CHIA SEEDS

flax

1 TEASPOON OF GROUND FLAX SEEDS

hemp

1 TEASPOON OF HEMP SEEDS

*you can make a smoothie bowl by using 1/3 cup instead of 1 cup of liquid

If you want to change some ingredients and create a different recipe, you can write the ingredient name on this side of the label and glue it to the recipe card on the next page

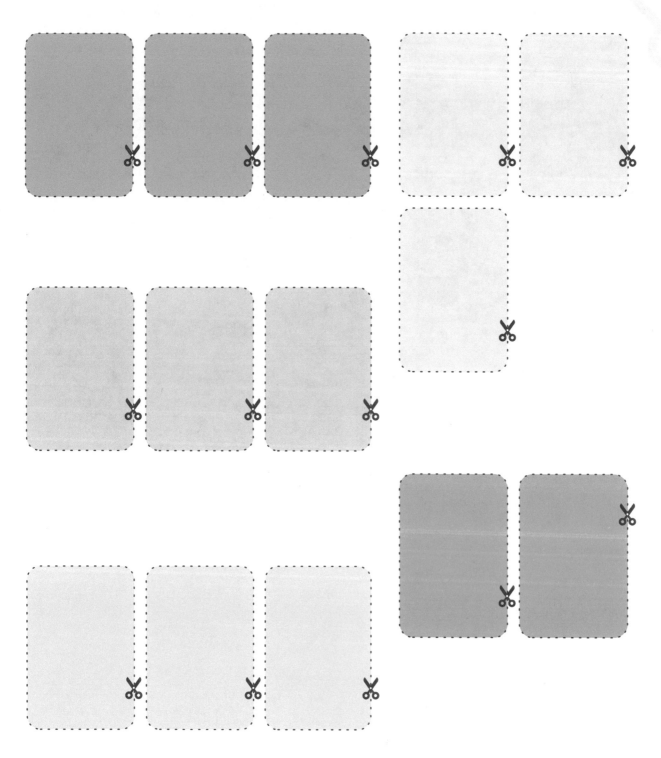

HOW TO USE?

Choose one of the ingredients from each color, cut it out, and place/glue it on the corresponding color below!

Read the instructions on the recipe card below, mix your chosen ingredients, and enjoy!

MY VITAMIN A
SUNSHINE SMOOTHIE!

 **ONE SERVING**

choose one:
LIQUID

A
choose one:
VITAMIN A

choose one:
BASE

choose one:
FLAVOR

Optional
choose one:
HEALTHY FATS

DID YOU KNOW?

Drinking one serving of this smoothie will give you half of the vitamin A you need for the entire day!

1. Place all ingredients in a blender.

2. Blend until smooth.

3. Adjust taste or texture, if needed (add more sweetener, spices or more liquid).

4. Pour into glass and enjoy!

DID YOU KNOW?

Vitamin A is a fat-soluble nutrient and gets absorbed better when you eat it with fat. You can make your smoothies even healthier by adding seeds, which can help your body absorb Vitamin A more effectively!

Circle ingredients you have chosen! Color your Vitamin A smoothie!

MY VITAMIN A SMOOTHIE

Plant Powered
B VITAMINS
NUTRITION EDUCATION FOR KIDS

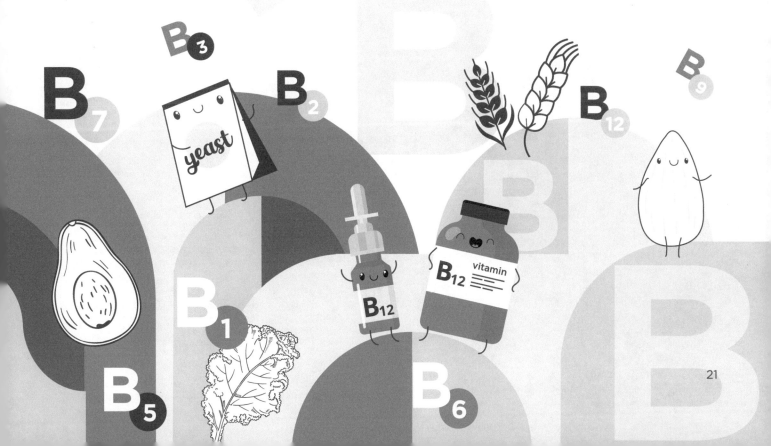

THERE ARE 8 B VITAMINS

THAT HELP TO PRODUCE ENERGY FROM FOODS WE EAT

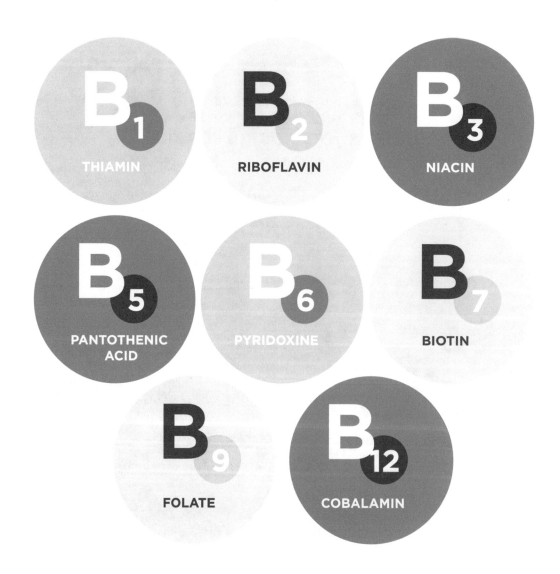

B1 THIAMIN

B2 RIBOFLAVIN

B3 NIACIN

B5 PANTOTHENIC ACID

B6 PYRIDOXINE

B7 BIOTIN

B9 FOLATE

B12 COBALAMIN

THE HEALTH BENEFITS OF
B VITAMINS

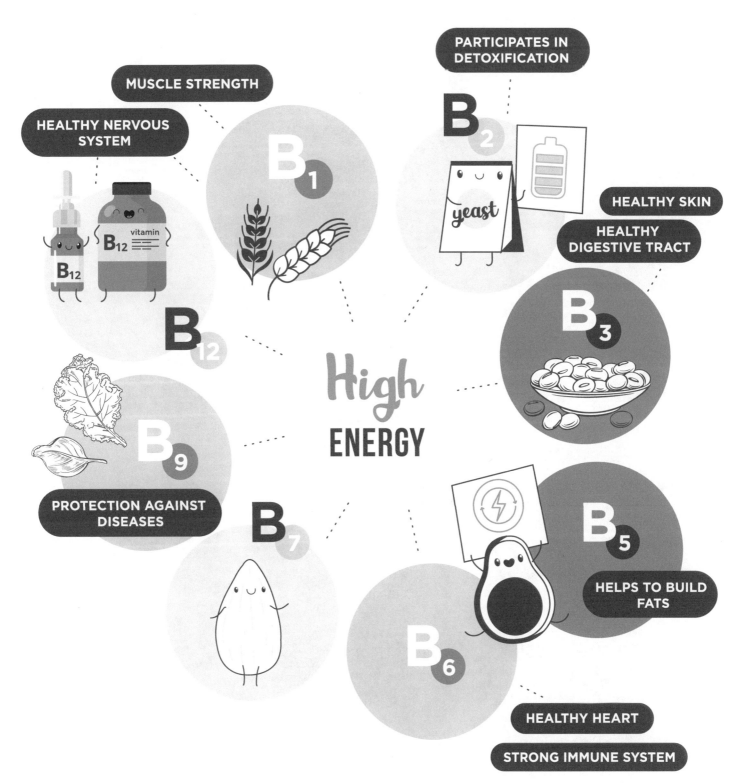

PARTICIPATES IN DETOXIFICATION

MUSCLE STRENGTH

HEALTHY NERVOUS SYSTEM

B1

B2

yeast

HEALTHY SKIN

HEALTHY DIGESTIVE TRACT

B3

B12

B12

vitamin

B12

High
ENERGY

B9

PROTECTION AGAINST DISEASES

B7

B5

HELPS TO BUILD FATS

B6

HEALTHY HEART

STRONG IMMUNE SYSTEM

COLOR
B VITAMINS FOODS!

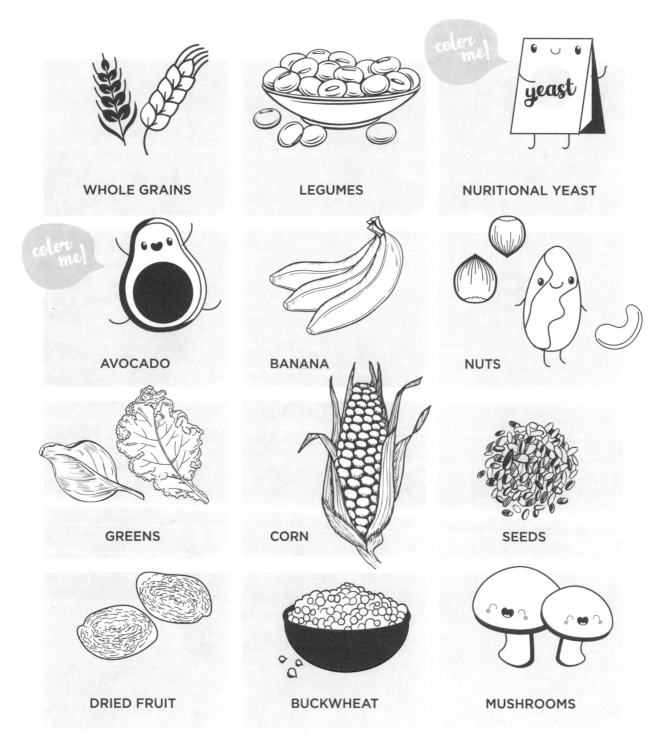

WHOLE GRAINS

LEGUMES

color me!

yeast

NURITIONAL YEAST

color me!

AVOCADO

BANANA

NUTS

GREENS

CORN

SEEDS

DRIED FRUIT

BUCKWHEAT

MUSHROOMS

Create your own B Vitamins pancakes by choosing one ingredient of each color! Pick all your chosen ingredients and combine them on the recipe card (next page)!

choose one
PICK YOUR LIQUID*:

1 CUP SOY MILK

1 CUP OTHER PLANT MILK

1 CUP ALMOND MILK

choose one
PICK YOUR SOURCE OF B VITAMINS:

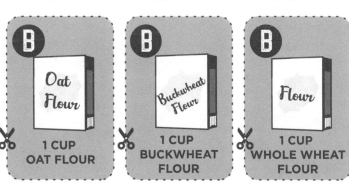

1 CUP OAT FLOUR

1 CUP BUCKWHEAT FLOUR

1 CUP WHOLE WHEAT FLOUR

choose one
PICK YOUR BASE*:

1/2 CUP MASHED OVERRIPE BANANA

1/2 CUP APPLE SAUCE

1/2 CUP PLANT BASED YOGURT

choose one
PICK YOUR TASTE:

1 TEASPOON CINNAMON

1 TEASPOON VANILLA EXTRACT

1 TABLESPOON CACAO POWDER

choose one:
SWEETEN IT UP:

1 TABLESPOON DATE PASTE

1 TABLESPOON DATE SYRUP

1 TABLESPOON MAPLE SYRUP

If you want to change some ingredients and create a different recipe, you can write the ingredient name on this side of the label and glue it to the recipe card on the next page

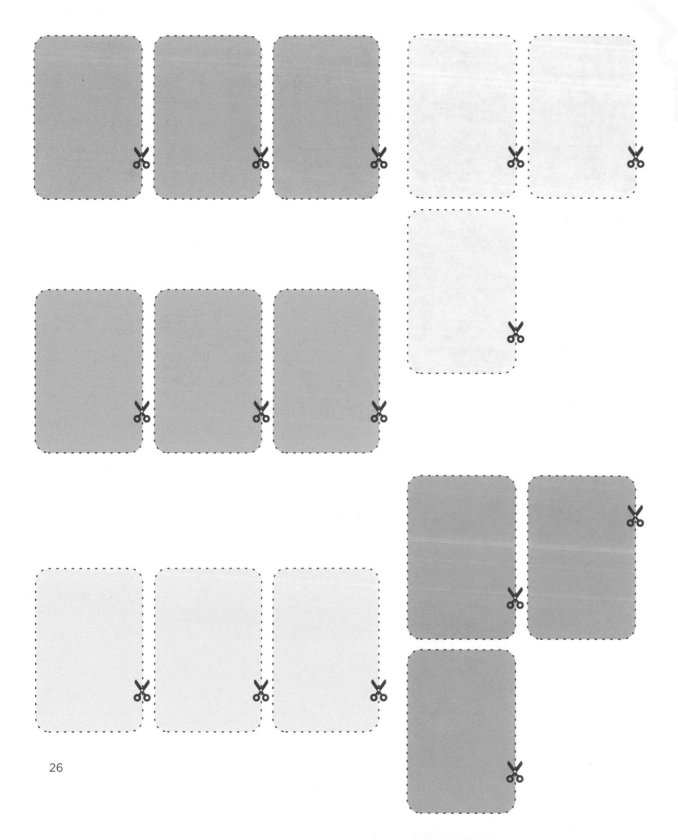

HOW TO USE?

Choose one of the ingredients from each color, cut it out, and place/glue it on the corresponding color below!

Read the instructions on the recipe card below, mix your chosen ingredients, and enjoy!

MY B VITAMINS
PANCAKES!

choose one:
LIQUID

B

choose one:
B VITAMINS

choose one:
BASE

choose one:
FLAVOR

choose one:
SWEETENER

1. Place all wet ingredients in a big bowl. Mix well.
2. Add all of the remaining ingredients and stir until you get a smooth batter.
3. If the batter seems too runny, let the mixture sit for ~3 minutes to thicken.
*You can also use a blender to mix all of the ingredients together.
4. Preheat a non-stick pan over medium heat, add a little bit of oil.
5. When hot, add batter to the pan. Use the back of your spoon to shape the batter into round pancakes.
6. Cook until there are bubbles around the edges and they have lightly browned.
7. Flip and cook until the other side is completely cooked.
8. Add your desired toppings, and enjoy!

DID YOU KNOW?

Whole grains have a much higher amount of B vitamins compared to refined grains like white flour and white pasta. This is because B vitamins are found in the outer layer of a grain. Refined grains have this outer layer removed, resulting in a loss of B vitamins.

MY B VITAMINS PANCAKES

WHERE TO FIND
VITAMIN B₁₂

B₁₂
COBALAMIN

BENEFITS OF VITAMIN B12:

- high energy
- healthy nervous system
- healthy heart

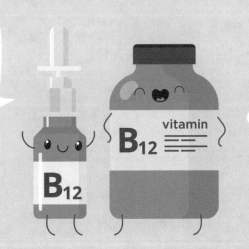

VITAMIN B₁₂ SUPPLEMENTS

VITAMIN B12 FORTIFIED FOODS

Adding vitamins to foods is called "fortifying"

Almond milk

Soy milk

fortified with VITAMIN B₁₂

Plant yoghurt

fortified with VITAMIN B 12

VEGGIE BURGER

Breakfast cereal

fortified with VITAMIN B12

GRAINS THAT CONTAIN
B VITAMINS

Let's explore some grains high in B vitamins: brown rice, whole wheat, oats, buckwheat, millet, whole barley, and quinoa. These grains are excellent sources of B vitamins, which are important for your health and energy.

THERE ARE TWO TYPES OF GRAINS: WHOLE GRAIN AND REFINED GRAIN.

Whole grain products have all the parts of the grain, including the outer layer and core, where most of the B vitamins are found. Refined grains, on the other hand, have had these parts removed, resulting in very few B vitamins.

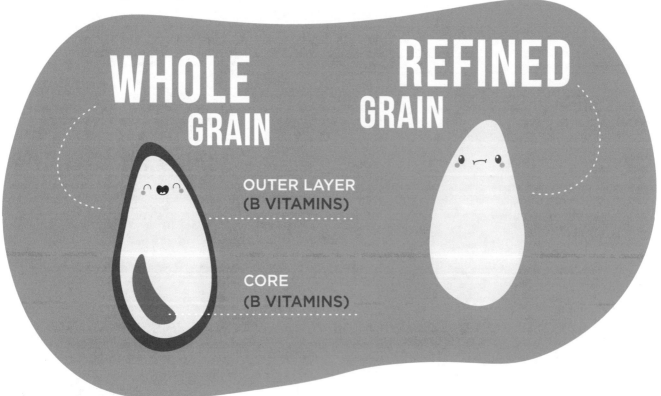

So, remember to choose whole grain options like brown rice, whole wheat, oats, buckwheat, millet, whole barley, and quinoa for a healthy dose of B vitamins! They'll help you stay strong and energetic.

Plant Powered
VITAMIN C
NUTRITION EDUCATION FOR KIDS

FUN EXERCISES | ALL ABOUT VITAMIN C | VITAMIN C SMOOTHIE RECIPE

The Health Benefits of
VITAMIN C

DID YOU KNOW?

Vitamin C is a special vitamin that doesn't like heat. It can easily get lost when we cook our food. That's why raw fruits and veggies have more Vitamin C than the ones we cook.

STRONG

IMMUNE SYSTEM

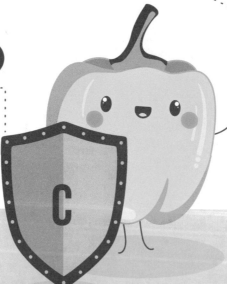

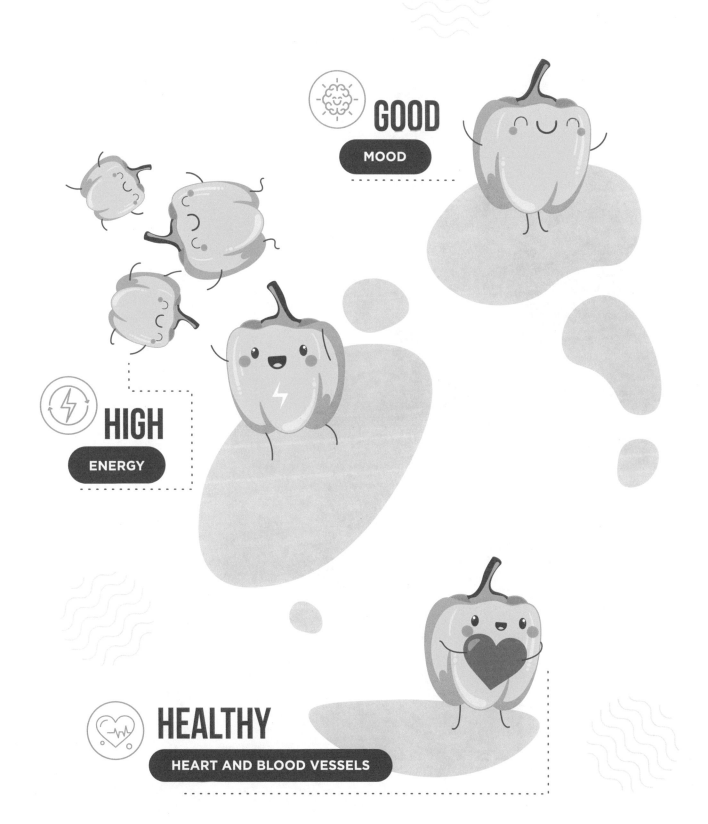

GOOD
MOOD

HIGH
ENERGY

HEALTHY
HEART AND BLOOD VESSELS

FOODS THAT CONTAIN
VITAMIN C

TOP 5

1. **BELL PEPPERS (RED, YELLOW)**
2. **BLACK CURRANTS**
3. **KIWI**
4. **KALE**
5. **ORANGE**

COLOR
VITAMIN C FOODS

PINEAPPLE

STRAWBERRIES

color me!

GRAPEFRUIT

RED CABBAGE

RAW PEAS

CANTALOUPE

PAPAYA

PARSLEY

POMEGRANATE

color me!

BROCCOLI

color me!

BRUSSELS SPROUTS

TOMATO

HOW MUCH
IN ONE DAY?

YOU CAN GET THE VITAMIN C NECESSARY FOR THE DAY IF YOU EAT ONE OF THESE:

1/2 CUP
BLACK CURRANTS

or

1 CUP RAW PEAS

or

Choose one:

or

1 MEDIUM
BELL PEPPER

1/2 CUP KIWI

or

or

1 MEDIUM ORANGE

CUSTOMIZE YOUR OWN VITAMIN C SMOOTHIE!

Create your own Vitamin C smoothie by choosing one ingredient of each color! Pick all your chosen ingredients and combine them on the recipe card (next page)!

choose one
PICK YOUR LIQUID*:

1 CUP APPLE JUICE

1 CUP ORANGE JUICE

1 CUP PINEAPPLE JUICE

choose one
PICK YOUR VITAMIN C:

1/2 CUP BLACK CURRANTS

1/2 CUP STRAWBERRIES

1/2 CUP FROZEN KIWI

choose one
PICK YOUR BASE*:

1/2 CUP FROZEN BANANA

1/2 CUP FROZEN MANGO

1/2 CUP FROZEN PINEAPPLE

choose one
SWEETEN IT UP:

3 - 4 SMALL DATES

1 TABLESPOON DATE SYRUP

*you can make a smoothie bowl by using 1/3 cup instead of 1 cup of liquid

If you want to change some ingredients and create a different recipe, you can write the ingredient name on this side of the label and glue it to the recipe card on the next page

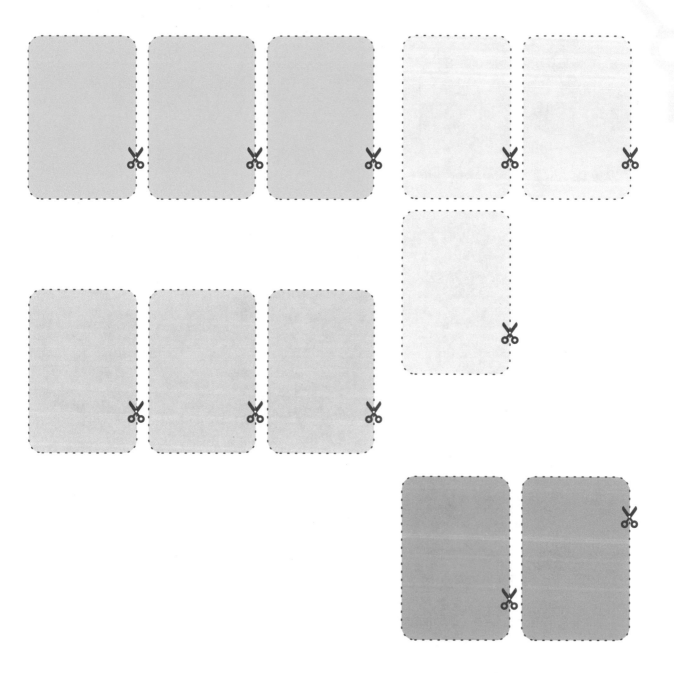

HOW TO USE?

Choose one of the ingredients from each color, cut it out, and place/glue it on the corresponding color below!

Read the instructions on the recipe card below, mix your chosen ingredients, and enjoy!

MY VITAMIN C SMOOTHIE!

 ONE SERVING

choose one: LIQUID	C choose one: VITAMIN C	choose one: BASE	choose one: SWEETENER

DID YOU KNOW?

Some more, some less, but ALL raw fruits and vegetables contain Vitamin C!

1. Place all ingredients in a blender.

2. Blend until smooth.

3. Adjust taste or texture, if needed (add more sweetener, spices or more liquid).

4. Pour into glass and enjoy!

DID YOU KNOW?

Vitamin C has another superpower! It helps your body absorb a special mineral called iron. Iron is really important because it helps you grow and stay healthy. So, when you eat foods rich in Vitamin C along with plant-based foods, it helps your body get all the iron it needs to keep you strong!

Circle ingredients you have chosen! Color your Vitamin C smoothie!

MY VITAMIN C SMOOTHIE

Plant Powered
VITAMIN D
NUTRITION EDUCATION FOR KIDS

FUN EXERCISES | ALL ABOUT VITAMIN A | SUNSHINE SMOOTHIE RECIPE

The Health Benefits of
VITAMIN D

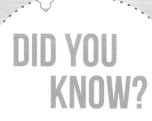

DID YOU KNOW?

Vitamin D also helps keep your heart healthy, which is like a strong and powerful engine in your body.

MAINTAINING

HEALTHY BONES

OVERALL

HEALTH

STRONG

IMMUNE SYSTEM

WHERE CAN YOU FIND
VITAMIN D?

DID YOU KNOW?

Your skin can make vitamin D when it gets sunlight! But remember, don't spend too much time in the sun. The sun's rays can be strong and sometimes cause your skin to get sunburned. That's why it's a great idea to take care of your skin by wearing clothes with long sleeves and a hat, and by finding a shady spot when you're outside. So, enjoy the sun, but always remember to be kind to your skin and keep it safe!

EXPOSURE TO THE SUN ON A REGULAR BASIS

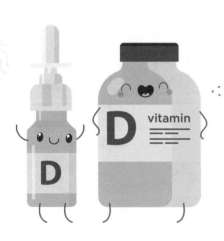

HOW MUCH IN 1 DAY?

It's hard to get enough vitamin D from the sun if you spend lots of time indoors. Ask your doctor if you need a vitamin D supplement!

- **VITAMIN D SUPPLEMENTS**

- **VITAMIN D FORTIFIED FOODS**

fortified with VITAMIN D

Plant milk

Fruit juice

fortified with VITAMIN D

Breakfast cereal

fortified with VITAMIN D

Plant yoghurt

43

FIND THE BEST WAY TO
VITAMIN D!

Vitamin D has a special superpower! It helps our bodies absorb calcium from the foods we eat.
Help calcium rich foods meet vitamin D!

CALCIUM

START

VITAMIN D

Here are some calcium rich plant-based foods

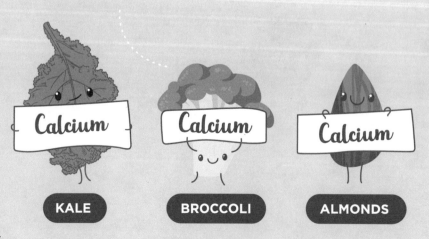

Calcium

Calcium

Calcium

KALE

BROCCOLI

ALMONDS

DID YOU KNOW?

Calcium is like the building blocks for our bones and teeth, and Vitamin D makes sure we get enough of it. So, with the help of Vitamin D, our bodies can stay strong, and our bones can grow healthy!

CALCIUM AND
VITAMIN D

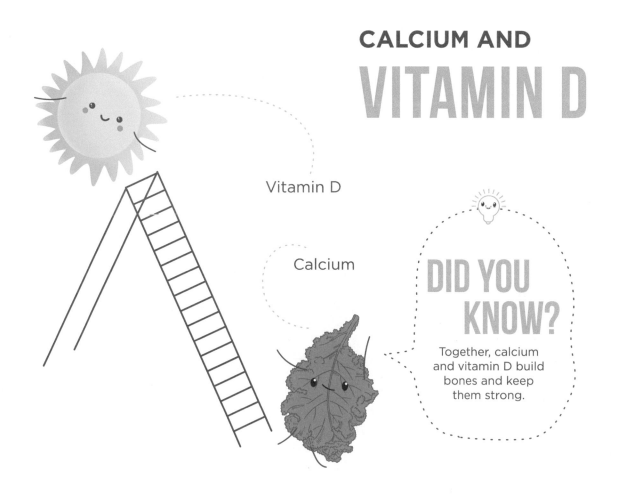

Vitamin D

Calcium

DID YOU KNOW?

Together, calcium and vitamin D build bones and keep them strong.

Let's find and circle some foods that are rich in calcium and need the superpower of Vitamin D to be absorbed better! Remember to use the hints from the previous page to help you out.

Spot at least
10 DIFFERENCES!

WHY DO YOU THINK KALE, ALMOND, AND BROCCOLI
LOOK DIFFERNT WHEN GETTING SUNLIGHT?

Plant Powered
VITAMIN E
NUTRITION EDUCATION FOR KIDS

FUN EXERCISES | ALL ABOUT VITAMIN E | VITAMIN E MIKSHAKE RECIPE

The Health Benefits of
VITAMIN E

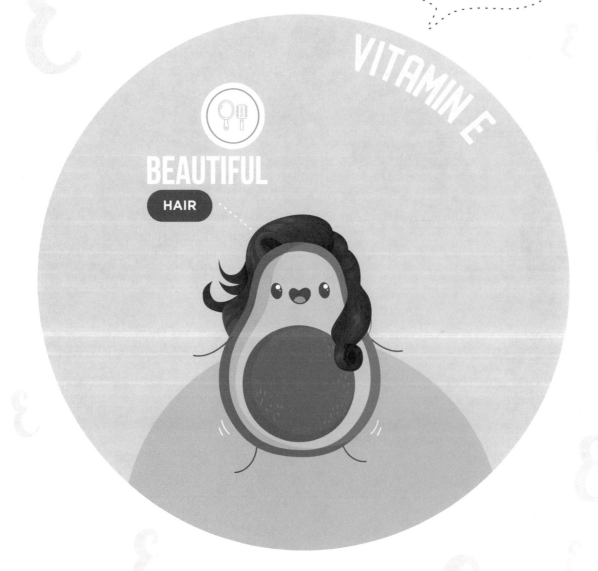

VITAMIN E

BEAUTIFUL

HAIR

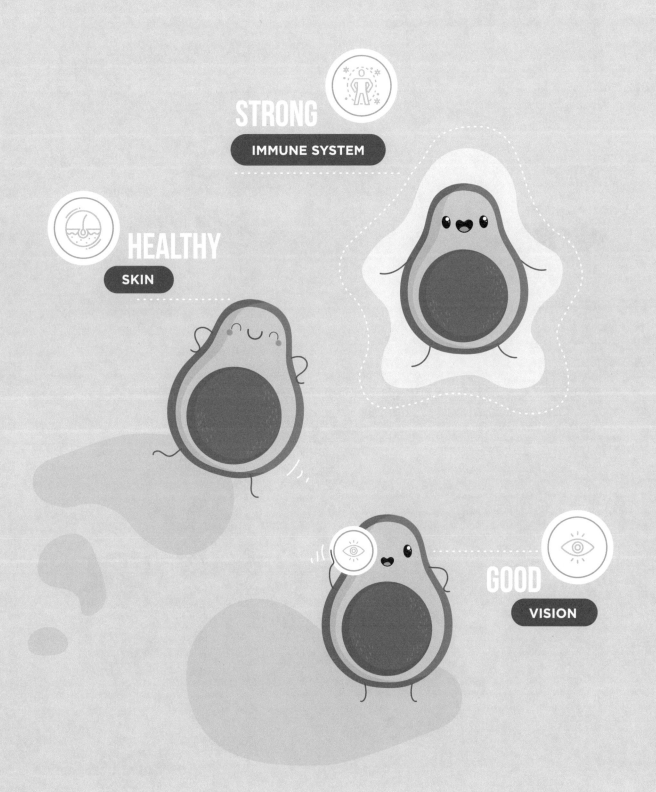

STRONG
IMMUNE SYSTEM

HEALTHY
SKIN

GOOD
VISION

FOODS THAT CONTAIN
VITAMIN E

TOP 5

1 SUNFLOWER SEEDS (OR SUNFLOWER SEED BUTTER)

2 ALMONDS

3 HAZELNUTS

4 AVOCADO

5 PEANUTS (OR PEANUT BUTTER)

peanut butter

VITAMIN E FOODS

BROCCOLI

CARROTS

color me!

KIWI

PEACHES

WHOLE GRAINS

DANDELION GREENS

OLIVES

APRICOTS

MANGO

color me!

BRAZIL NUTS

SPINACH

TAHINI
(sesame seed butter)

How much
IN ONE DAY?

You get your vitamin E necessary for the day if you eat one of these:

Choose one:

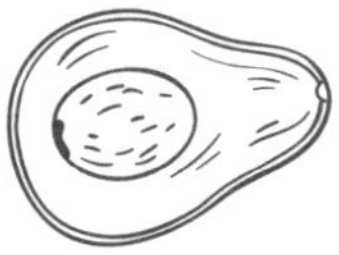

half an
avocado

\+

3 tabelspoons
sunflower seeds

or

1/4 cup
almonds

\+

2 tabelspoons of
tahini (sesame seed butter)

or

1/3 cup
hazelnuts

\+

one mango

\+

one kiwi

Create your own Vitamin E milkshake by choosing one ingredient of each color! Pick all your chosen ingredients and combine them on the recipe card (next page)!

CUSTOMIZE YOUR OWN VITAMIN E MILKSHAKE!

choose one:
PICK YOUR LIQUID*:

1 CUP SOY MILK

1 CUP OTHER PLANT MILK

1 CUP ALMOND MILK

choose one:
PICK YOUR VITAMIN E:

E **1-2 TBSP ALMOND BUTTER**

E **1-2 TBSP PEANUT BUTTER**

E **2 TBSP SUNFLOWER SEEDS**

choose one:
PICK YOUR BASE*:

1/2 CUP FROZEN BANANA

1/4 CUP CASHEWS + 1/2 CUP ICE CUBES

1/2 CUP ROLLED OATS + 1/2 CUP ICE CUBES

optional:
BOOST YOUR SMOOTHIE WITH MORE VITAMIN E:

E **1/2 CUP CHOPPED SPINACH**

E **1/2 CUP CHOPPED DANDELION GREENS**

E **1 CUP FROZEN AVOCADO**

E **1 CUP CHOPPED KALE**

choose one:
SWEETEN IT UP:

3-4 SMALL DATES

1 TABLESPOON DATE SYRUP

*you can make a smoothie bowl by using 1/3 cup instead of 1 cup of liquid

If you want to change some ingredients and create a different recipe, you can write the ingredient name on this side of the label and glue it to the recipe card on the next page

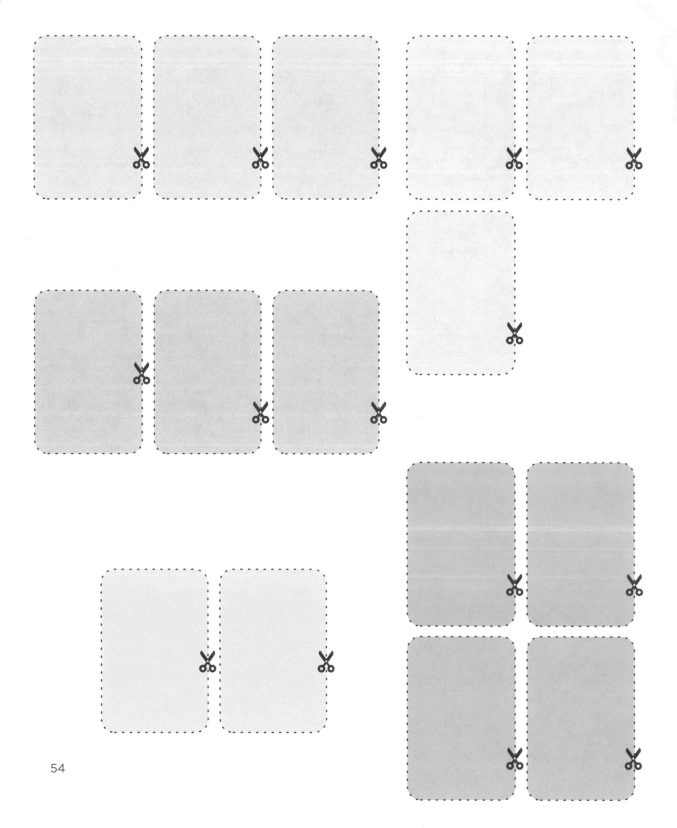

HOW TO USE?

Choose one of the ingredients from each color, cut it out, and place/glue it on the corresponding color below!

Read the instructions on the recipe card below, mix your chosen ingredients, and enjoy!

MY VITAMIN E
MILKSHAKE!

 ONE SERVING

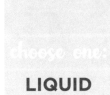

choose one:	choose one:	choose one:	choose one:
LIQUID	**VITAMIN E**	**BASE**	**SWEETENER**

Optional

choose one:

MORE VITAMIN E

1. Place all ingredients in a blender.

2. Blend until smooth.

3. Adjust taste or texture, if needed (add more sweetener, spices or more liquid).

4. Pour into glass and enjoy!

Color your Vitamin E milkshake!

MY VITAMIN E MILKSHAKE

Plant Powered
VITAMIN K
NUTRITION EDUCATION FOR KIDS

The Health Benefits of VITAMIN K

DID YOU KNOW?

Vitamin K is like a superhero for your bones! It helps your body build strong bones by making sure calcium goes to the right places. Vitamin K helps regulate the levels of calcium in your blood and makes sure it goes into your bones where it's needed the most. So, don't forget to eat foods rich in calcium to keep your bones strong and healthy!

 ## STRONG BONES

DEFENSE AT TIMES OF INJURY

ENSURES BLOOD CLOTTING IN CASE OF BLEEDING

FOODS THAT CONTAIN
VITAMIN K

TOP 5

1 PARSLEY

2 KALE

3 DANDELION GREENS

4 SPINACH

5 COLLARD GREENS

COLOR
K VITAMIN FOODS!

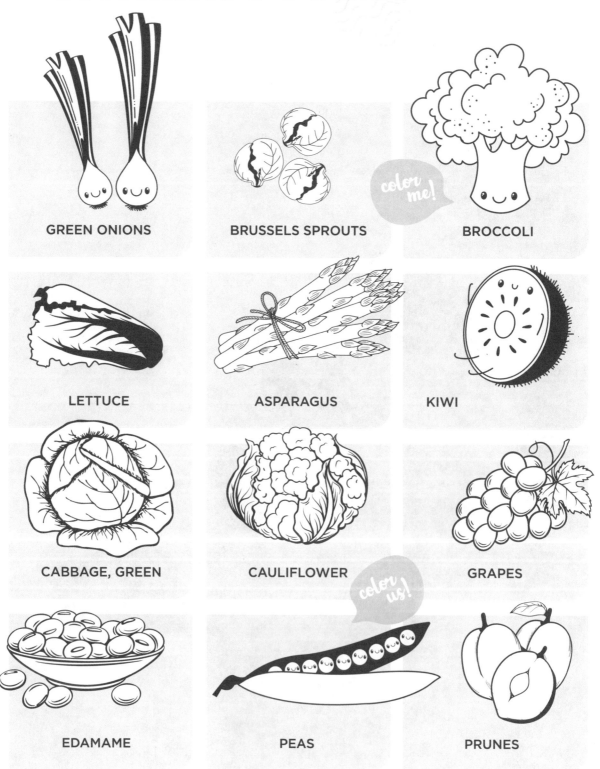

GREEN ONIONS

BRUSSELS SPROUTS

color me!

BROCCOLI

LETTUCE

ASPARAGUS

KIWI

CABBAGE, GREEN

CAULIFLOWER

GRAPES

color us!

EDAMAME

PEAS

PRUNES

Create your own Vitamin K smoothie by choosing one ingredient of each color! Pick all your chosen ingredients and combine them on the recipe card (next page)!

CUSTOMIZE
YOUR OWN VITAMIN K
GREEN POWER SMOOTHIE!

choose one
PICK YOUR LIQUID*:

✂ **1 CUP APPLE JUICE** ✂ **1 CUP COCONUT WATER**

✂ **1 CUP PINEAPPLE JUICE**

choose one
PICK YOUR VITAMIN K:

✂ **1/2 CUP SPINACH** ✂ **1/2 CUP KALE (STEMS REMOVED)** ✂ **1/2 CUP DANDELION GREENS**

choose one
PICK YOUR BASE*:

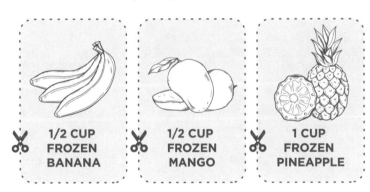

✂ **1/2 CUP FROZEN BANANA** ✂ **1/2 CUP FROZEN MANGO** ✂ **1 CUP FROZEN PINEAPPLE**

choose one
SWEETEN IT UP:

✂ **3 - 4 SMALL DATES** ✂ **1 TABLESPOON DATE SYRUP**

optional:
BOOST YOUR SMOOTHIE
WITH HEALTHY FATS:

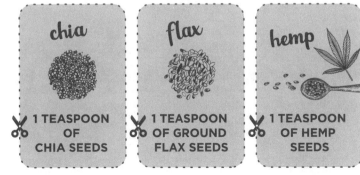

chia *flax* *hemp*

✂ **1 TEASPOON OF CHIA SEEDS** ✂ **1 TEASPOON OF GROUND FLAX SEEDS** ✂ **1 TEASPOON OF HEMP SEEDS**

*you can make a smoothie bowl by using 1/3 cup instead of 1 cup of liquid

If you want to change some ingredients and create a different recipe, you can write the ingredient name on this side of the label and glue it to the recipe card on the next page

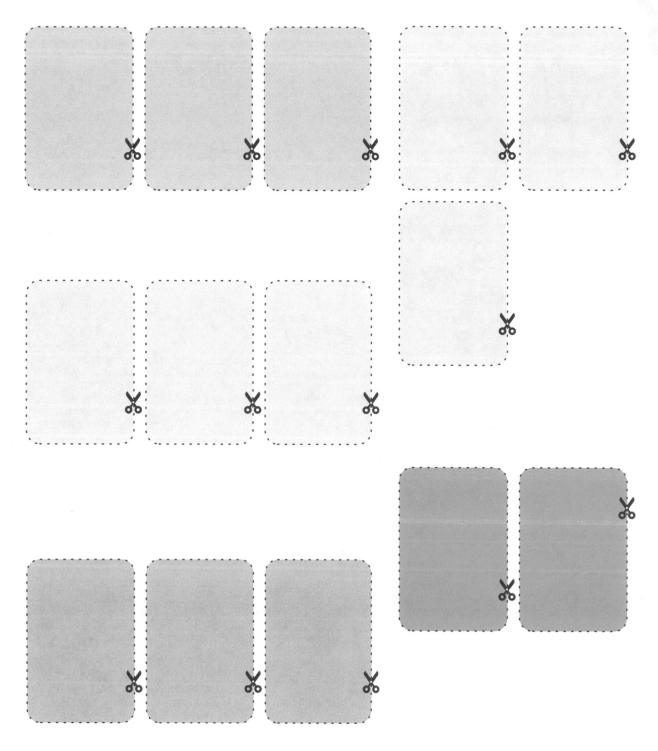

HOW TO USE?

Choose one of the ingredients from each color, cut it out, and place/glue it on the corresponding color below!

Read the instructions on the recipe card below, mix your chosen ingredients, and enjoy!

MY VITAMIN K
GREEN POWER SMOOTHIE!

 ONE SERVING

choose one:

LIQUID

K

choose one:

VITAMIN K

choose one:

BASE

choose one:

SWEETENER

Optional

choose one:

HEALTHY FATS

If you are not used to the taste of greens in your smoothie, you can add less than ½ a cup of greens at first!

1. Place all ingredients in a blender.

2. Blend until smooth.

3. Adjust taste or texture, if needed (add more sweetener, spices or more liquid).

4. Pour into glass and enjoy!

COLOR
YOUR VITAMIN K SMOOTHIE!

MY VITAMIN K SMOOTHIE

HOW MUCH
IN ONE DAY?

YOU CAN GET THE VITAMIN K NECESSARY FOR
THE DAY IF YOU EAT ONE OF THESE:

K
2 TABLESPOONS OF
KALE

or

K
1 TABLESPOON OF
PARSLEY

or

Choose one:

or

K
1/3 CUP COOKED
BRUSSEL SPROUTS

K
1 MEDIUM KIWI

or

or

K
1/3 CUP COOKED
BROCCOLI

HOW MANY VITAMIN K-RICH

spinach leaves can you collect by choosing the shortest way through the maze? Color the leaves you have collected along the way!

CIRCLE ONE PRODUCT FOR EACH VITAMIN!

VITAMIN A
good vision

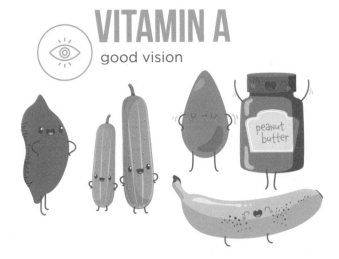

VITAMIN E
healthy hair and skin

VITAMIN C
strong immune system

VITAMIN K
defense at times of injury

B VITAMINS
high energy

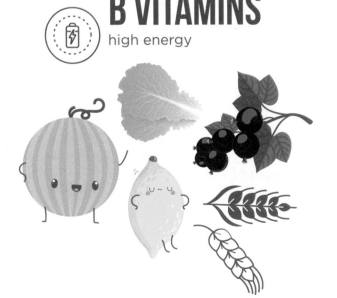

VITAMIN D
overall health

WHICH VITAMIN GIVES YOU WHICH BENEFIT? FIND THE RIGHT WAY!

VITAMIN A   VITAMIN C   B VITAMINS

GOOD **VISION**

HIGH ENERGY

STRONG **IMMUNE SYSTEM**

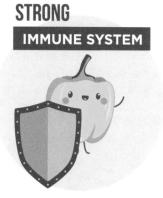

OVERALL HEALTH

BEAUTIFUL **HAIR**

STRONG BONES

VITAMIN E   VITAMIN K   VITAMIN D

COLOR THESE FOODS AND PAIR THEM WITH THE RESPONDING VITAMIN!

GREEN OLIVES

ALMONDS

AVOCADO

BROWN BEANS

SWEET POTATOES

VITAMIN E

B VITAMINS

VITAMIN A

VITAMIN K

SPINACH

PARSLEY

SQUASH

CARROTS

WHOLE GRAINS

KALE

WHICH FOOD CONTAINS WHICH VITAMIN?

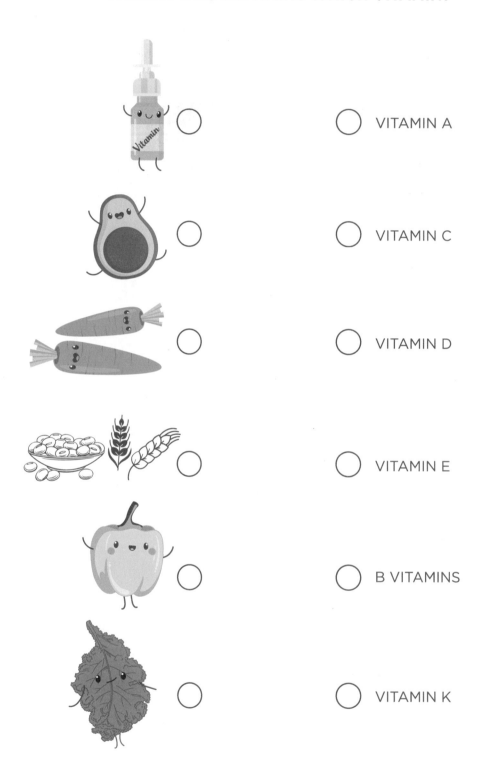

VITAMIN A

VITAMIN C

VITAMIN D

VITAMIN E

B VITAMINS

VITAMIN K

Fill in the crossword and find the letters!

1	2	3	4	5	6	7	8

THE RIGHT ANSWERS

EXERCISE 1

VITAMIN K > Parsley

VITAMIN D > the sun

B VITAMINS > whole grains

VITAMIN A > sweet potato,

VITAMIN C > bell pepper,

VITAMIN E > sunflower seeds

EXERCISE 2

VITAMIN A > Carrot - Good vision

B VITAMINS > Yeast - High energy

VITAMIN C > Yellow bell pepper -

Strong immune system

VITAMIN E > Avocado - Beautiful hair

VITAMIN K > Kale - Strong bones

VITAMIN D > Sun - Overall health

EXERCISE 3

VITAMIN A - orange:

Carrot

Sweet potato

Butternut squash

VITAMIN K - dark green:

Kale

Spinach

Parsley

VITAMIN E - light green

Avocado

Green olives

VITAMIN B - brown:

Whole grains

Brown beans

Almonds

EXERCISE 4

VITAMIN A > Carrot

B VITAMINS > Legumes and whole grains

VITAMIN C > Yellow bell pepper

VITAMIN D > Supplement

VITAMIN E > Avocado

VITAMIN K > Kale

EXERCISE 5

1 -Broccoli
2 - Tomato
3 - Lime
4 - Banana
5 - Apple
6 - Avocado
7 - Cherries
8 - Yeast
9 - Orange

The hidden word - Vitamins

Congratulations
ON COMPLETING OUR BOOK!

IF YOU WANT TO MAKE LEARNING EVEN MORE AWESOME, CHECK OUT OUR FREE COURSES: "ALL ABOUT VITAMINS" AND "ALL ABOUT MINERALS."

Go to **https://www.youtube.com/@nutriedukids/playlists**

WHY YOU'LL LOVE OUR COURSES:

- **Fun Videos:** Watch visually engaging animations and lessons that make learning about vitamins and minerals super interesting.
- **Book in Action:** See all the information from the book come to life! Our videos help kids remember essential information with visuals.

REINFORCE YOUR KNOWLEDGE GAINED DURING THE COURSE WITH OUR PRINTABLE ACTIVITY PAGES, WHICH ARE BOTH FUN AND EDUCATIONAL!

Supercharge your child's learning with our bundle! Get printable activities for "All About Vitamins" and "All About Minerals" YouTube courses, along with a kid-friendly cookbook featuring matching recipes for a fun kitchen experience!

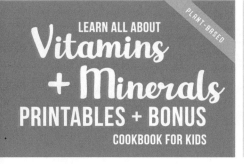

Go to **https://www.nutriedukids.com/ebooks-for-kids**

nutri·edu·kids
WWW.NUTRIEDUKIDS.COM

ALL FEEDBACK IS GREATLY APPRECIATED!

For any inquiries please feel free to email us at:

hello@nutriedukids.com

Want a freebie? Join our newsletter and get a free gift at:

www.nutriedukids.com

For references, please visit - https://www.nutriedukids.com/references

Made in United States
Troutdale, OR
12/03/2024

25784170R00042